Contents

Designed, pieced, and appliquéd by Mary Hickey; quilted by Dawn Kelly

Quilt size: 35" x 35" • Block size: 5" x 5"

Baby Bows and Twinkle Toes

Shiny new Mary Janes skip between the bows and dance across the quilt top. They're a breeze to fuse to the background, and you can stitch them in place with a straight, zigzag, or blanket stitch.

Materials

Yardage is based on 42"-wide fabric.

¾ yard *total* of assorted white-and-red prints for background

⅓ yard *total* of assorted red prints for bow ties and shoe linings

½ yard of red print for outer border

⅓ yard of white-and-red striped fabric for inner border

¼ yard of black print for shoes

⅜ yard of black polka-dot print for binding

1¼ yards of fabric for backing

40" x 40" square of batting

½ yard of paper-backed fusible web

Cutting

All measurements include ¼"-wide seam allowances. Cut strips across the fabric width.

From the assorted red prints, cut *8 matching sets* of:
2 squares, 2½" x 2½" (16 total)
2 squares, 1½" x 1½" (16 total)

From the assorted white-and-red prints, cut a total of:
17 squares, 5½" x 5½"
8 *matching sets of 2* squares, 2½" x 2½" (16 total)

From the remainder of the assorted white-and-red prints, cut *8 matching sets* of:
1 rectangle, 1½" x 4½" (8 total)
1 rectangle, 1½" x 5½" (8 total)

From the white-and-red striped fabric, cut:
4 strips, 2" x 42"

From the red print for outer border, cut:
4 strips, 4" x 42"

From the black polka-dot print, cut:
4 strips, 2½" x 42"

Making the Bow Tie Blocks

1 Using a pencil and ruler, draw a diagonal line from corner to corner on the wrong side of each assorted red 1½" square. Place a square on one corner of each assorted white-and-red 2½" square. Sew on the marked lines, trim ¼" from the stitching lines, flip the triangles open, and press.

2 Sew two matching squares from step 1 and the two matching assorted red 2½" squares from the same set together to make a bow-tie unit. Add an assorted white-and-red 1½" x 4½" rectangle to the right side of the unit and the matching 1½" x 5½" rectangle to the bottom of the unit to complete the block. Repeat to make a total of eight Bow Tie blocks.

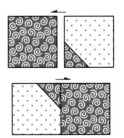

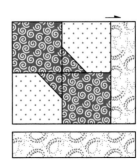 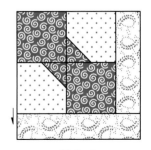

Make 8.

Assembling the Quilt Top

1 Refer to the quilt assembly diagram below to arrange the blocks and assorted white-and-red 5½" squares into five rows, orienting the Bow Tie blocks as shown. Sew the squares in each row together, and then sew the rows together.

2 Measure the quilt top for borders. Sew the white-and-red striped 2"-wide inner-border strips to the quilt top. Repeat for the red 4"-wide outer-border strips. Press all seam allowances outward.

3 Following the manufacturer's instructions, use fusible web to make the shoe and shoe-lining appliqué shapes below and appliqué them to the quilt top. Refer to the photo on page 4 for placement as needed. Stitch around the shapes by hand or machine using a straight, zigzag, or blanket stitch.

Finishing the Quilt

For more details on quilting and finishing, go to ShopMartingale.com/HowtoQuilt.

1 Cut the backing fabric so it's approximately 4" to 6" larger than the quilt top.

2 Layer the backing, batting, and quilt top and baste the layers together.

3 Hand or machine quilt as desired. The quilt shown was machine quilted with scrolled feathers through the blocks and spirals in the borders.

4 Trim the batting and backing fabric so the edges are even with the quilt-top edges. Attach a hanging sleeve, if desired, and then bind the quilt using the black polka-dot strips. Add a label.

Quilt assembly

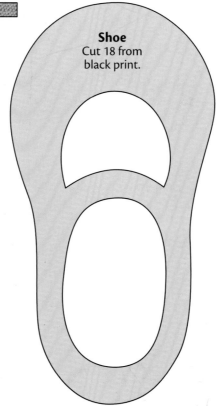

Shoe
Cut 18 from black print.

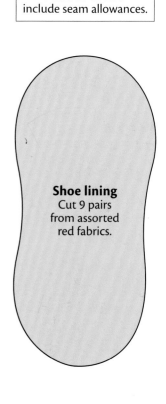

Shoe lining
Cut 9 pairs from assorted red fabrics.

Patterns do not include seam allowances.

Small Checks

These delightful blocks are energetic, easy to piece, and visually stimulating. Any conversation or theme print that you can cut into 6" to 7½" squares can be used for this quilt.

Materials

Yardage is based on 42"-wide fabric.

⅞ yard of bright-pink print for Small Checks blocks and outer border
1 yard of theme print for alternate blocks
⅜ yard of pink-dotted print for Small Checks blocks
⅓ yard of white print for Small Checks blocks
¼ yard of brown print for inner border *gRay*
½ yard of dark-pink print for binding *l·me*
1¾ yards of fabric for backing *e*
48" x 48" square of batting

Cutting

All measurements include ¼"-wide seam allowances.
Cut strips across the fabric width.

From the white print, cut:
6 strips, 1½" x 42"

From the bright-pink print, cut:
6 strips, 1½" x 42"
5 strips, 3½" x 42"   *border 2*

From the pink-dotted print, cut:
2 strips, 5½" x 42"; crosscut into 13 squares,
    5½" x 5½"

From the theme print, fussy cut:
12 squares, 7½" x 7½"

From the brown print, cut:
4 strips, 1½" x 42"   *2 ½ Border 2*

From the dark-pink print, cut:
5 strips, 2½" x 42"

Bind   3 ½ out

Making the Small Checks Blocks

1 Stitch three white and two bright-pink 1½" x 42" strips together as shown to make strip set A. Crosscut the strip set into 26 segments, 1½" wide.

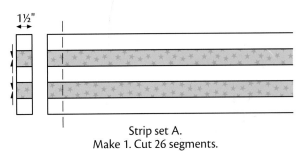

Strip set A.
Make 1. Cut 26 segments.

2 Stitch three white and four bright-pink 1½" x 42" strips together as shown to make strip set B. Crosscut the strip set into 26 segments, 1½" wide.

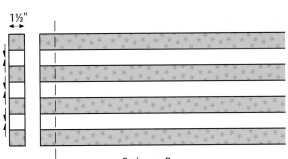

Strip set B.
Make 1. Cut 26 segments.

3 Sew a strip set A segment to the sides of each pink-dotted square. Add a strip set B segment to the top and bottom of each square.

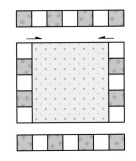 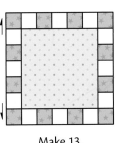

Make 13.

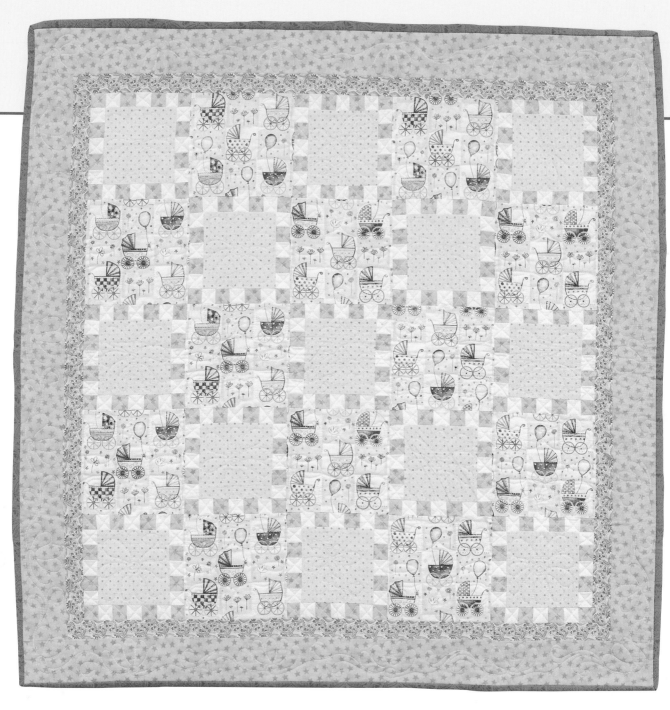

Designed and pieced by Mary Hickey; quilted by Dawn Kelly
Quilt size: 43" x 43" • **Block size:** 7" x 7"

Assembling the Quilt Top

1. Refer to the quilt assembly diagram below to arrange the Small Checks blocks and the theme-print 7½" blocks into five rows of five blocks each, alternating the blocks in each row and from row to row. Sew the blocks in each row together, and then sew the rows together.

2. Measure the quilt top for borders. Sew the brown 1½"-wide inner-border strips to the quilt top. Repeat with the bright-pink 3½"-wide outer-border strips, piecing the strips together as necessary to achieve the required length.

Finishing the Quilt

For more details on quilting and finishing, go to ShopMartingale.com/HowtoQuilt.

1. Cut the backing fabric so it's approximately 4" to 6" larger than the quilt top.

2. Layer the backing, batting, and quilt top and baste the layers together. Hand or machine quilt as desired.

3. Trim the batting and backing fabric so the edges are even with the quilt-top edges. Attach a hanging sleeve, if desired, and then bind the quilt using the dark-pink strips. Add a label.

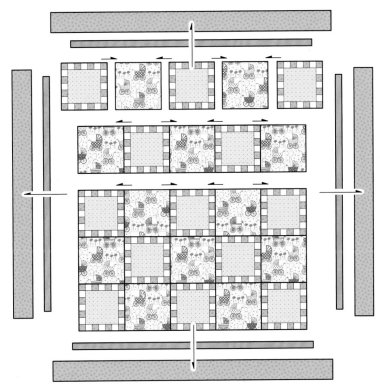

Quilt assembly

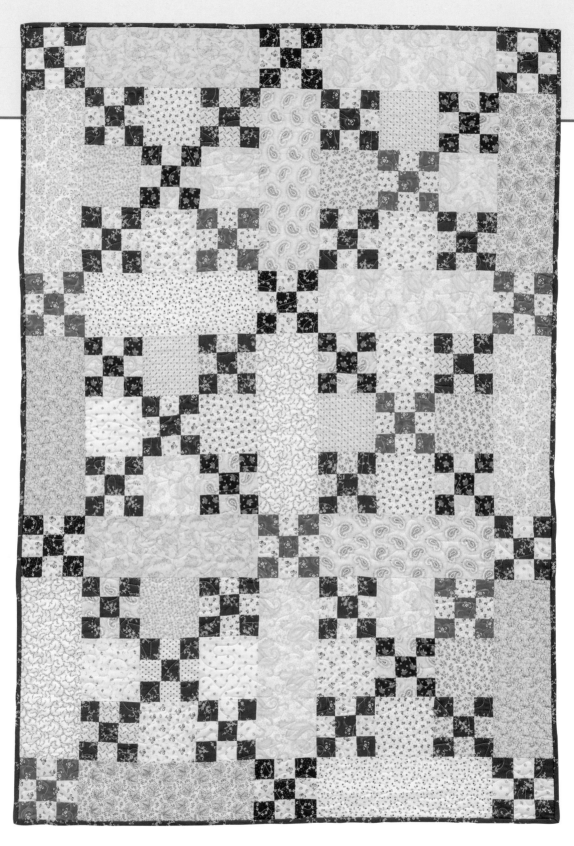

Designed and pieced by Nancy J. Martin; quilted by Shelly Nolte

Quilt size: 34¼" x 49¼" • **Block size:** 11¼" x 11¼"

Big Boy Blue

"Big Boy Blue" features a treasured Double Nine Patch design and classic blue-and-white color scheme. This quilt will have grandmas everywhere asking their little grandsons, "Who's my big boy?"

Materials

Yardage is based on 42"-wide fabric.

8 fat quarters of assorted light prints for blocks
    and sashing
8 fat quarters of assorted blue prints for blocks
    and sashing
⅜ yard of dark-blue print for binding
1⅝ yards of fabric for backing
38" x 53" piece of batting

Cutting

All measurements include ¼"-wide seam allowances.
Cut strips across the fabric width.

From *each* of the 8 fat quarters of assorted blue prints, cut:
2 strips, 1¾" x 21" (16 total)
1 strip, 1¾" x 10½" (8 total)

From *each* of the 8 fat quarters of assorted light prints, cut:
2 strips, 1¾" x 21" (16 total)
2 strips, 4¼" x 11¾". Cut one additional strip from one
    fat quarter (17 total).
3 squares, 4¼" x 4¼" (24 total)

From the dark-blue print, cut:
5 strips, 2¼" x 42"

Making the Nine-Patch Units and Blocks

1 Using the 1¾" x 21" strips, stitch two matching blue strips and one light strip together to make strip set A. Repeat to make a total of eight strip sets.

From each strip set, cut 10 segments, 1¾" wide. From two of the strip sets, cut two additional segments (84 total).

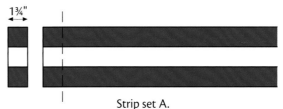

Strip set A.
Make 8. Cut 10 segments from each and 2
additional segments from two (84 total).

2 Cut the remaining light 1¾" x 21" strips in half crosswise. Using the same fabric combinations you used for the A strip sets, sew the light half strips and the blue 1¾" x 10½" strips together to make strip set B. From each strip set, cut five segments. Cut one additional segment from each of the two fabric combinations from which you cut the additional A segments (42 total).

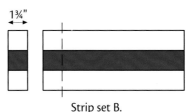

Strip set B.
Make 8. Cut 5 segments from each and 2
additional segments from two (42 total).

3 Using segments with the same fabric combinations, join two A segments and one B segment to make a nine-patch unit. Repeat to make a total of 42 nine-patch units.

Make 42.

11

4 Stitch five nine-patch units and four light 4¼" squares together to make a Double Nine Patch block. Repeat to make a total of six blocks.

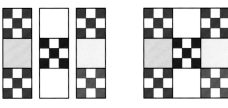

Make 6.

Assembling the Quilt Top

1 Join two blocks and three light 4¼" x 11¾" strips to make a block row. Repeat to make a total of three rows.

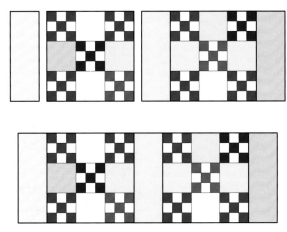

Make 3.

2 Join three of the remaining nine-patch units and two light 4¼" x 11¾" strips to make a sashing row. Repeat to make a total of four rows.

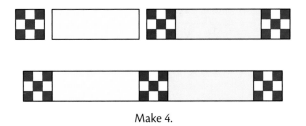

Make 4.

3 Join the block rows and the sashing rows, matching seams.

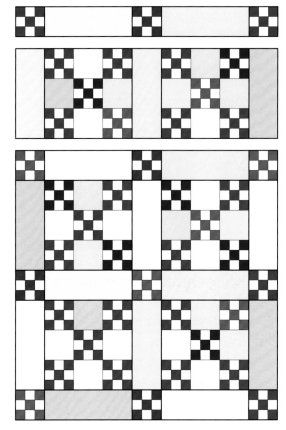

Quilt assembly

Finishing the Quilt

For more details on quilting and finishing, go to ShopMartingale.com/HowtoQuilt.

1 Cut the backing fabric so it's approximately 4" to 6" larger than the quilt top.

2 Layer the backing, batting, and quilt top and baste the layers together. Hand or machine quilt as desired.

3 Trim the batting and backing fabric so the edges are even with the quilt-top edges. Attach a hanging sleeve, if desired, and then bind the quilt using the dark-blue strips. Add a label.

Rolling Along

Use your favorite Jelly Roll to create this happy quilt. The Rolling Nine Patch blocks are easy to make, and the pieced border adds the perfect finishing touch.

Materials

Yardage is based on 42"-wide fabric.

1 Jelly Roll **OR** 40 assorted dark, medium, and light strips, 2½" x 42", for blocks, sashing squares, and outer border
¾ yard of white-on-white print for blocks and sashing
¼ yard of yellow-striped fabric for inner border
½ yard of light-green diagonally striped fabric for binding*
3 yards of fabric for backing
50" x 50" piece of batting

*If using straight-grain striped fabric, buy ¾ yard to make bias binding.

Cutting

All measurements include ¼"-wide seam allowances. Cut strips across the fabric width.

From the white-on-white print, cut:
5 strips, 2½" x 42"; crosscut into 72 squares, 2½" x 2½"
1 strip, 10½" x 42"; crosscut into 12 strips, 2½" x 10½"

From *each of 9* assorted dark Jelly Roll strips, cut:
6 rectangles, 2½" x 4½" (4 each for flying-geese units*, 2 each for border; 54 total)
5 squares, 2½" x 2½" (45 total)*

From *each of 7* assorted medium or dark Jelly Roll strips, cut:
12 squares, 2½" x 2½" (84 total)*
2 rectangles, 2½" x 4½" (14 total)

From *each of 3* assorted light Jelly Roll strips, cut:
12 squares, 2½" x 2 1/2" (36 total)*
2 rectangles, 2½" x 4½" (6 total)

From *each of 6* assorted light Jelly Roll strips, cut:
6 rectangles, 2½" x 4½" (36 total)

From *1* light Jelly Roll strip, cut:
8 squares, 2½" x 2½"

From the yellow-striped fabric, cut:
4 strips, 1½" x 42"

From the light-green diagonally striped fabric, cut:
5 strips, 2¼" x 42"

*Keep like fabrics together.

Making the Blocks

Each block uses the same dark fabric for the nine-patch unit and the flying-geese unit. Each block also uses one light print for the nine-patch unit.

1 Use a pencil to lightly draw a diagonal line from corner to corner on the wrong side of each white square. Place a marked square on one end of a dark rectangle, right sides together. Sew along the marked line and trim away the corner fabric, leaving a ¼" seam allowance. Press the seam allowances toward the resulting white triangle. In the same manner, sew a white square to the other end of the rectangle to complete a flying-geese unit. Make four matching units for each block (36 total).

Flying-geese unit.
Make 4 matching units
for each block (36 total).

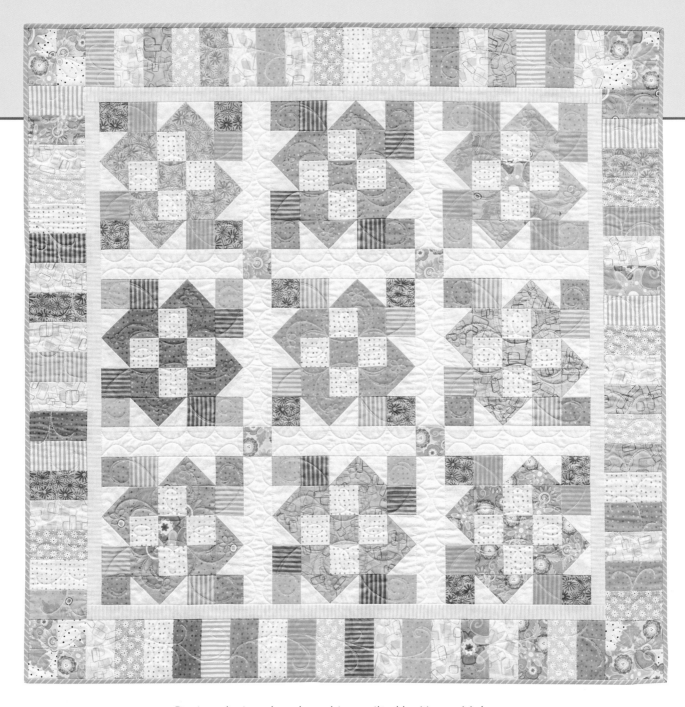

Designed, pieced, and machine quilted by Nancy Mahoney

Quilt size: 44½" x 44½" • **Block size:** 10" x 10"

2 Lay out five matching dark squares and four matching light squares in a nine-patch arrangement as shown. Sew the squares together into rows and press the seam allowances toward the light squares. Sew the rows together to complete the nine-patch unit. Press the seam allowances toward the center. Make nine units.

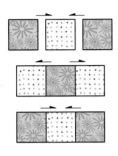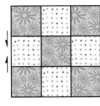

Nine-patch unit.
Make 9 total.

3 Using four matching medium/dark squares and four matching flying-geese units; sew a square to one end of each unit as shown, being careful to sew the square to the correct side of the flying-geese unit. Make four matching units for each block (36 total).

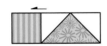

Make 4 matching units
for each block (36 total).

4 Lay out four matching medium/dark squares, four matching units from step 3, and one matching nine-patch unit from step 2 as shown. Sew the pieces together into rows and press the seam allowances as indicated. Sew the rows together to complete the block; press the seam allowances toward the center. Make nine blocks.

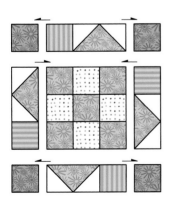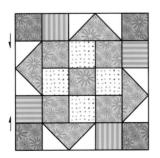

Make 9.

Assembling the Quilt Top

1 Lay out the blocks in three rows of three blocks each. Place white 2½" x 10½" sashing strips between the blocks and medium/dark 2½" sashing squares between the horizontal sashing strips, referring to the quilt assembly diagram on page 16. When you're pleased with the color arrangement, sew the blocks and sashing pieces into rows. Then sew the rows together. Press all seam allowances toward the sashing strips.

2 Measure the length of your quilt top; it should be 34½". If your top measures less than 33½" or more than 35½", you'll need to adjust the pieced borders in step 3 to fit. Trim two of the yellow strips to this length and sew them to the sides of the quilt top. Press the seam allowances toward the borders. Measure the width of your quilt top; it should be 36½". Trim the remaining two yellow strips to this length and sew them to the top and bottom of the quilt top.

3 For the outer border, randomly sew the medium/dark rectangles and light rectangles together in pairs. Make 36 pairs. You'll have two rectangles left over. Then sew nine pairs together to make a border strip as shown. Press all the seam allowances open to reduce bulk. Make four border strips.

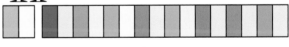

Make 4.

4 Sew two matching light squares and two matching medium/dark squares together to make a Four Patch block as shown. Make four.

Four-Patch block.
Make 4.

5 Sew border strips from step 3 to opposite sides of the quilt top as shown in the quilt assembly diagram. Press the seam allowances toward the inner border.

6 Sew the Four Patch blocks to both ends of the two remaining border strips and press the seam allowances toward the blocks. Then sew the borders to the top and bottom of the quilt top. Press the seam allowances toward the inner border.

Finishing the Quilt

For more details on quilting and finishing, go to ShopMartingale.com/HowtoQuilt.

1 Cut the backing fabric so it's approximately 4" to 6" larger than the quilt top.

2 Layer the backing, batting, and quilt top and baste the layers together. Hand or machine quilt as desired.

3 Trim the batting and backing fabric so the edges are even with the quilt-top edges. Attach a hanging sleeve, if desired, and then bind the quilt using the light-green strips. If you don't have a diagonally stripe fabric, you can achieve the same effect with straight-grain striped fabric and cutting bias binding. Add a label.

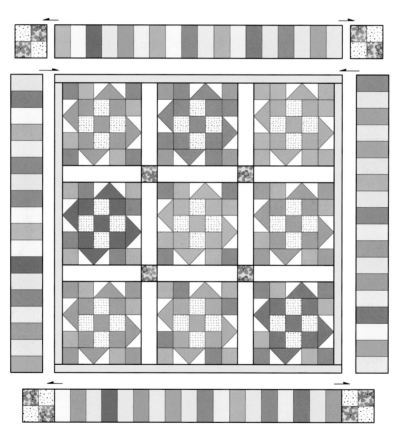

Quilt assembly

Sweet Rosebuds

This lovely quilt is the perfect gift for a sweet baby girl. By setting the five blocks on point, this became a somewhat larger quilt, making it nice for a toddler or to hang on a nursery wall.

Materials

Yardage is based on 42"-wide fabric.

2½ yards of white print for background
⅜ yard of medium-pink print for blocks
⅜ yard of green print for blocks
¼ yard of dark-pink mottled fabric for blocks
⅝ yard of green-and-pink print for binding
3 yards of fabric for backing
53" x 53" piece of batting

Cutting

All measurements include ¼"-wide seam allowances. Cut strips across the fabric width.

From the dark-pink mottled fabric, cut:
2 strips, 2½" x 42"; crosscut into 20 squares,
    2½" x 2½"

From the medium-pink print, cut:
4 strips, 2½" x 42"; crosscut into 60 squares,
    2½" x 2½"

From the green print, cut:
4 strips, 2½" x 42"

From the white print, cut:
1 square, 27" x 27"; cut into quarters diagonally to
    yield 4 side triangles
2 squares, 14" x 14"; cut in half diagonally to yield
    4 corner triangles
5 squares, 8½" x 8½"
2 strips, 4½" x 42"
5 strips, 2½" x 42"; crosscut into 20 pieces, 2½" x 8½"
2 strips, 1½" x 42"; crosscut into 4 pieces, 1½" x 16½"

From the green-and-pink print, cut:
2¼"-wide bias strips to equal 206" in length

Making the Blocks

After each sewing step, press the seam allowances as directed by the arrows in the illustration.

1 Sew 20 dark-pink squares to 20 medium-pink squares. Then sew the remaining medium-pink squares together in pairs. Sew the pairs into four-patch units as shown.

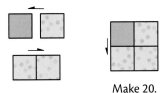

Make 20.

2 Sew a green strip to each side of a white 4½"-wide strip. Make two strip sets and cut 20 segments, 2½" wide.

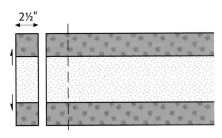

Make 2 strip sets.
Cut 20 segments.

3 Sew a segment from step 2 to each white 2½" x 8½" piece.

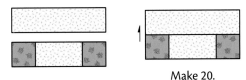

Make 20.

4 Sew a four-patch unit from step 1 to each end of 10 units from step 3 as shown.

Make 10.

Designed and pieced by Laurie Bevan; hand quilted by Virginia Lauth

Quilt size: 48½" x 48½" • **Block size:** 16" x 16"

5 Sew the remaining units from step 3, the units from step 4, and the white 8½" squares together as shown. Make five blocks.

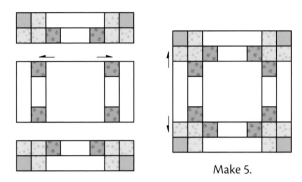

Make 5.

Assembling the Quilt Top

1 Sew a 16½"-long white piece to one side of four of the blocks.

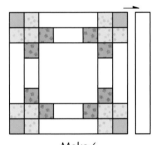

Make 4.

2 Lay out the pieced blocks and the side and corner triangles as shown. Sew the blocks and side triangles together in rows, and then sew the rows together. Add the corner triangles last.

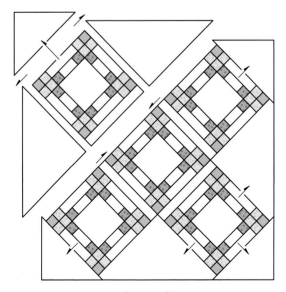

Quilt assembly

3 Trim the edges of the quilt top, leaving 1" of white print beyond the block points. Square up the four corners. The rosebud blocks will appear to float on the background.

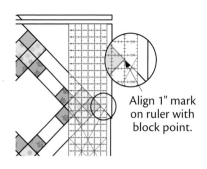

Align 1" mark on ruler with block point.

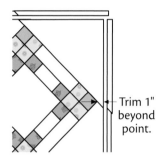

Trim 1" beyond point.

Finishing the Quilt

For more details on quilting and finishing, go to ShopMartingale.com/HowtoQuilt.

1 Piece the backing fabric so it's approximately 4" to 6" larger than the quilt top.

2 Layer the backing, batting, and quilt top and baste the layers together. Hand or machine quilt as desired.

3 Trim the batting and backing fabric so the edges are even with the quilt-top edges. Attach a hanging sleeve, if desired, and then bind the quilt the green-and-pink 2¼"-wide bias strips. Add a label.

Designed by Mary Hickey, pieced by Cleo Nollette, and quilted by Frankie Schmitt

Quilt size: 29½" x 35¼" • **Block size:** 5¾" x 5¾"

Petite Trellis

Repeating one simple block creates the illusion of a trellis in this remarkably clever little quilt. This quilt is just the right size for the serious work of cuddling, burping, drooling, and all-around comforting.

Materials

Yardage is based on 42"-wide fabric.

½ yard of blue butterfly print for outer border
⅓ yard of light-blue print for blocks
⅓ yard of medium-blue print for blocks
⅓ yard of white tone-on-tone print for blocks
¼ yard of light-green print for blocks
¼ yard of medium-green print for blocks
¼ yard of blue-and-lime-green print for inner border
⅜ yard of light-lime-green print for binding
1¼ yards of fabric for backing
34" x 40" piece of batting
Square rotary-cutting ruler

Cutting

All measurements include ¼"-wide seam allowances.
Cut strips across the fabric width.

From *each* of the light-blue and medium-blue prints, cut:
4 strips, 1½" x 42" (8 total)
1 strip, 2¼" x 42"; crosscut into 10 squares, 2¼" x 2¼".
   Cut each square in half diagonally to yield 20
   triangles (40 total).

From the white tone-on-tone print, cut:
2 strips, 4" x 42"; crosscut into 20 squares, 4" x 4".
   Cut each square into quarters diagonally to yield
   80 triangles.

From *each* of the medium-green and light-green prints, cut:
4 strips, 1½" x 42" (8 total)

From the blue-and-lime-green print, cut:
4 strips, 1" x 42"

From the blue butterfly print, cut:
4 strips, 3¼" x 42"

From the light-lime-green print for binding, cut:
4 strips, 2½" x 42"

Making the Trellis Blocks

1 Sew each medium-blue 1½" x 42" strip to a light-blue 1½" x 42" strip to make four strip sets. Press the seam allowances open. Crosscut the strip sets into 20 segments, 7¼" wide.

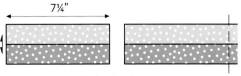

Make 4 strip sets.
Cut 20 segments.

2 Fold each segment in half crosswise, wrong sides together. Place your rotary-cutting ruler as close as possible to the folded edge; cut off the fold. With the trimmed pairs still layered, align the 45° angle of a square ruler with the seam line of the top segment and place the ruler corner just barely below the top of the segments. Cut along the angled edges of the ruler to create 20 mirror-image pairs.

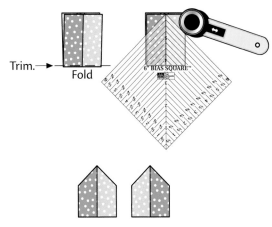

Make 20 pairs.

3 Sew a white triangle to both straight sides of each blue segment.

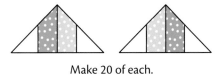

Make 20 of each.

4 Sew each medium-green 1½" x 42" strip to a light-green 1½" x 42" strip to make four strip sets. Crosscut the strip sets into 20 segments, 6⅝" wide.

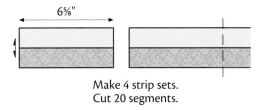

Make 4 strip sets.
Cut 20 segments.

5 Sew a light-blue triangle and a medium-blue triangle to each green segment as shown.

6 Sew together two blue units (make sure they're mirror images of each other) and one green unit to complete the block. Repeat to make a total of 20 blocks.

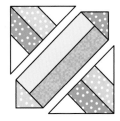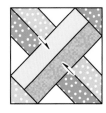

Make 20.

Assembling the Quilt Top

1 Refer to the quilt assembly diagram above right to carefully arrange the blocks into five rows of four blocks each. The blocks must be positioned the same in each row in order for the trellis design to form. Carefully pin and sew the blocks in each row together, and then pin and sew the rows together.

2 Measure the quilt top for borders. Sew the blue-and-lime-green 1"-wide inner-border strips to the quilt top. Repeat for the butterfly-print 3¼"-wide outer-border strips.

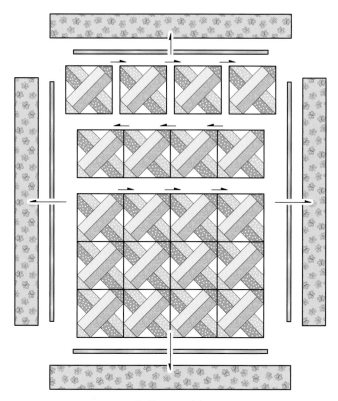

Quilt assembly

Finishing the Quilt

For more details on quilting and finishing, go to ShopMartingale.com/HowtoQuilt.

1 Cut the backing fabric so it's approximately 4" to 6" larger than the quilt top.

2 Layer the backing, batting, and quilt top and baste the layers together. Hand or machine quilt as desired.

3 Trim the batting and backing fabric so the edges are even with the quilt-top edges. Attach a hanging sleeve, if desired, and then bind the quilt with the light-lime-green strips. Add a label.

Little Dominoes

This quilt has fun written all over it! Pick a light fabric with lots of bright colors printed on it for the background and pair it with light- and medium-value prints of four coordinating colors.

Materials

Yardage is based on 42"-wide fabric.

¼ yard *each* of light-green, medium-green, light-blue, medium-blue, light-yellow, and medium-yellow prints

¾ yard of white star print for setting squares and triangles

⅝ yard of light-pink print for blocks and outer border

⅜ yard of medium-pink print for blocks and inner border

½ yard of dark-pink print for binding

1½ yards of fabric for backing

40" x 48" piece of batting

Cutting

All measurements include ¼"-wide seam allowances. Cut strips across the fabric width.

From the light-pink print, cut:
2 strips, 2" x 42"
4 strips, 3¾" x 42"

From the medium-pink print, cut:
2 strips, 2" x 42"
4 strips, 1½" x 42"

From *each* of the light-green, medium-green, light-blue, medium-blue, light-yellow, and medium-yellow prints, cut:
2 strips, 2" x 42" (12 total)

From the white star print, cut:
1 strip, 6½" x 42"; crosscut into 6 squares, 6½" x 6½"
1 strip, 9¾" x 42"; crosscut into 3 squares, 9¾" x 9¾".
   Cut each square into quarters diagonally to yield 12 side setting triangles (you'll have 2 left over).
1 strip, 5¼" x 42"; crosscut into 2 squares, 5¼" x 5¼".
   Cut each square in half diagonally to yield 4 corner setting triangles.

From the dark-pink print, cut:
5 strips, 2½" x 42"

Making the Dominoes Blocks

1 Stitch light-pink and medium-pink 2" x 42" strips together to make a strip set. Repeat to make a total of two strip sets. Crosscut the strip sets into 12 segments, 3½" wide. Repeat with the light-green and medium-green strips, the light-blue and medium-blue strips, and the light-yellow and medium-yellow strips.

Make 2 strip sets each of pink, green, blue, and yellow.
Cut 12 segments of each color.

2 Arrange one segment of each color into two horizontal rows of two segments each. The orientation of the segments doesn't have to be the same for each block, but the segments should alternate direction around the block. Sew the segments in each row together, and then sew the rows together. Repeat to make a total of 12 blocks.

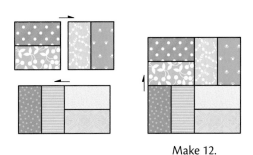

Make 12.

Designed and pieced by Mary Hickey; quilted by Julie Goodwin

Quilt size: 35" x 42½" • **Block size:** 6" x 6"

Assembling the Quilt Top

1 Refer to the quilt assembly diagram below to arrange the Dominoes blocks, the white 6½" squares, and the white star print side setting triangles into diagonal rows. Sew the pieces in each row together, and then sew the rows together, adding the corner setting triangles last.

2 Measure the quilt top for borders. Sew the medium-pink 1½"-wide inner-border strips to the quilt top. Repeat with the light-pink 3¾"-wide outer-border strips. Press all seam allowances outward.

Finishing the Quilt

For more details on quilting and finishing, go to ShopMartingale.com/HowtoQuilt.

1 Cut the backing fabric so it's approximately 4" to 6" larger than the quilt top.

2 Layer the backing, batting, and quilt top and baste the layers together. Hand or machine quilt as desired.

3 Trim the batting and backing fabric so the edges are even with the quilt-top edges. Attach a hanging sleeve, if desired, and then bind the quilt using the dark-pink 2½"-wide strips. Add a label.

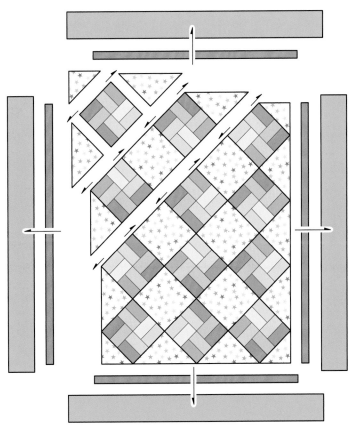

Quilt assembly

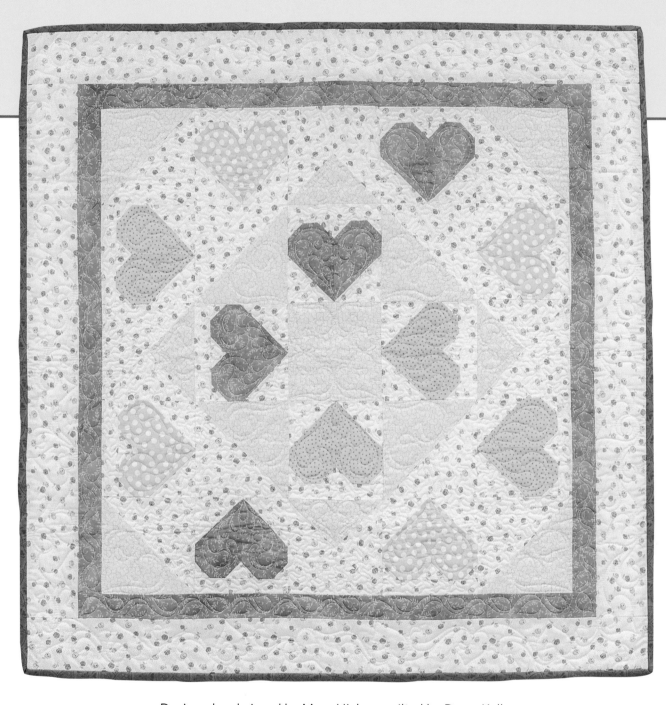

Designed and pieced by Mary Hickey; quilted by Dawn Kelly

Quilt size: 39" x 39" • **Block size:** 6" x 6"

Tender Hearts

Adorable Heart blocks are easily made with simple folded corners. Light pink triangles form a diamond shape around the little Heart blocks, adding interest and depth to the quilt without adding difficulty.

Materials

Yardage is based on 42"-wide fabric.

1⅜ yards of white print for block backgrounds and outer border
½ yard of dark-pink print for hearts and inner border
½ yard of pale-pink print for blocks
¼ yards *each* of 2 assorted pink prints for hearts
½ yard of dark-red print fabric for binding
1½ yards of fabric for backing
43" x 43" square of batting

Cutting

All measurements include ¼"-wide seam allowances.
Cut strips across the fabric width.

From the white print, cut:
3 strips, 3½" x 42"; crosscut into 24 squares, 3½" x 3½"
2 strips, 1½" x 42"; crosscut into 48 squares, 1½" x 1½"
2 strips, 1½" x 42"; crosscut into 12 rectangles,
   1½" x 6½"
1 strip, 7¼" x 42"; crosscut into 1 square, 7¼" x 7¼".
   Trim the remainder of the strip to 7" wide and
   crosscut into 4 squares, 7" x 7".
1 strip, 7" x 42"; crosscut into 2 squares, 7" x 7". Cut
   each square in half diagonally to yield 4 triangles.
4 strips, 3½" x 42"

From the dark-pink print, cut:
4 strips, 2" x 42"
2 strips, 3½" x 42"; crosscut into 8 rectangles,
   3½" x 5½"

From *each* of the 2 assorted pink prints, cut:
2 strips, 3½" x 42"; crosscut into 8 rectangles,
   3½" x 5½" (16 total)

From the pale-pink print, cut:
1 strip, 7" x 42"; crosscut into 4 squares, 7" x 7"
1 square, 6½" x 6½"
1 square, 7¼" x 7¼"

From the dark-red print, cut:
5 strips, 2½" x 42"

Making the Heart Blocks

1 Using a pencil and ruler, draw a diagonal line from corner to corner on the wrong side of each white 1½" square. Place two marked squares on each dark-pink and assorted pink 3½" x 5½" rectangle as shown. Sew on the marked lines, trim ¼" from the stitching lines, flip the white triangles open, and press.

Make 24.

2 Draw a diagonal line from corner to corner on the wrong side of each white 3½" square. Select two matching rectangles from step 1 and place a marked square on each rectangle, positioning the marked lines so they go in opposite directions on each rectangle as shown. Sew, trim, and press as before. Repeat with the remaining rectangles from step 1.

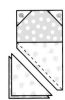 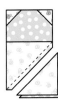 

Make 12 pairs.

3 Sew the matching units from step 2 together to make a heart unit.

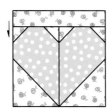

4 Sew a white 1½" x 6½" rectangle to the top of each heart unit to complete the blocks.

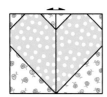

Make 12.

Making the Triangle Units

1 Mark a diagonal line on the wrong side of four white 7" squares. Place each square right sides together with a pale-pink 7" square. Sew ¼" from each side of the marked lines and cut the squares apart to make eight half-square-triangle units. Press. Trim each unit to 6½" square.

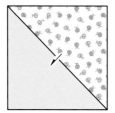

Make 8.

2 To make the split triangle units, repeat step 1 using the white and the pale-pink 7¼" squares to make two half-square-triangle units, but do not trim them. Cut each unit in half diagonally to make a pieced triangle.

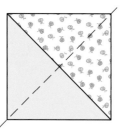
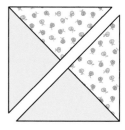

3 Sew a white triangle to each pieced triangle from step 2. Trim the blocks to 6½" square.

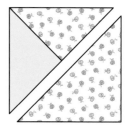
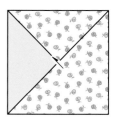

Make 4.

Assembling the Quilt Top

1 Refer to the quilt assembly diagram below to arrange the blocks, triangle units, and pale-pink 6½" square into five rows of five blocks each. Be sure each block is oriented as shown. Sew the blocks in each row together, and then sew the rows together.

2 Measure the quilt top for borders. Sew the dark-pink 2"-wide inner-border strips to the quilt top. Repeat with the white 3½"-wide outer-border strips.

Finishing the Quilt

For more details on quilting and finishing, go to ShopMartingale.com/HowtoQuilt.

1 Cut the backing fabric so it's approximately 4" to 6" larger than the quilt top.

2 Layer the backing, batting, and quilt top and baste the layers together. Hand or machine quilt as desired.

3 Trim the batting and backing fabric so the edges are even with the quilt-top edges. Bind the quilt with the dark red strips. Add a label.

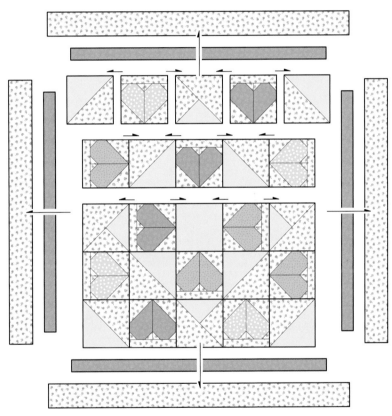

Quilt assembly

Designed and pieced by Mary Hickey; quilted by Dawn Kelly

Quilt size: 40" x 40" • **Block size:** 5" x 5"

Spring Mist

The delicate greens and soft blues of spring create a soothing wash of colors in this quilt made of a simple pieced block. By using scraps, you can add interest and translucency to the blocks.

Materials

Yardage is based on 42"-wide fabric.

¾ yard *total* of assorted light-blue prints for blocks
¾ yard *total* of assorted light-green prints for blocks
⅝ yard of medium-blue print for outer border
⅓ yard of light-blue print for inner border
¼ yard *total* of assorted medium-blue prints
    for blocks
¼ yard *total* of assorted medium-green prints
    for blocks
½ yard of medium-green print for binding
1¾ yards of fabric for backing
45" x 45" square of batting

Cutting

All measurements include ¼"-wide seam allowances.
Cut strips across the fabric width.

From *each* of 1 assorted light-blue and 1 assorted light-green print, cut:
2 squares, 5½" x 5½" (4 total)

From the assorted light-blue and light-green prints, cut:
16 *pairs* of matching squares of each color, 3" x 3"
    (32 of each color; 64 total)
16 squares of each color, 3½" x 3½" (32 total)

From the assorted medium-blue and medium-green prints, cut:
16 squares of each color, 3½" x 3½" (32 total)

From the light-blue print for inner border, cut:
4 strips, 2" x 42"

From the medium-blue print for outer border, cut:
4 strips, 4" x 42"

From the medium-green print for binding, cut:
5 strips, 2½" x 42"

Making the Blocks

1. Layer each light-blue 3½" square with a medium-blue 3½" square, right sides together and with the light blue square on top. Using a pencil and a rotary-cutting ruler, draw a diagonal line from corner to corner on the wrong side of the light-blue squares. Stitch ¼" from each side of the marked line. Cut the squares apart on the marked line to yield 32 half-square-triangle units. Repeat with the light-green and medium-green 3½" squares. Trim each unit to 3" x 3".

Make 32.   Make 32.

2. Sew together two matching blue half-square-triangle units and two matching light-blue 3" squares. Repeat to make a total of 16 blue blocks. Repeat with the green half-square-triangle units and light-green 3" squares to make a total of 16 green blocks.

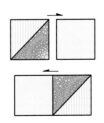

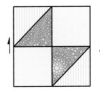

Make 16.   Make 16.

Assembling the Quilt Top

1 Refer to the quilt assembly diagram below to arrange the blocks and squares into six rows of six blocks each. Be sure the blocks are oriented as shown. Sew the pieces in each row together, and then sew the rows together.

2 Measure the quilt top for borders. Sew the light-blue 2"-wide inner-border strips to the quilt top. Repeat for the medium-blue 4"-wide outer-border strips.

Finishing the Quilt

For more details on quilting and finishing, go to ShopMartingale.com/HowtoQuilt.

1 Piece the backing fabric so it's approximately 4" to 6" larger than the quilt top.

2 Layer the backing, batting, and quilt top and baste the layers together. Hand or machine quilt as desired.

3 Trim the batting and backing fabric so the edges are even with the quilt-top edges. Attach a hanging sleeve, if desired, and then bind the quilt using the medium-green binding strips. Add a label.

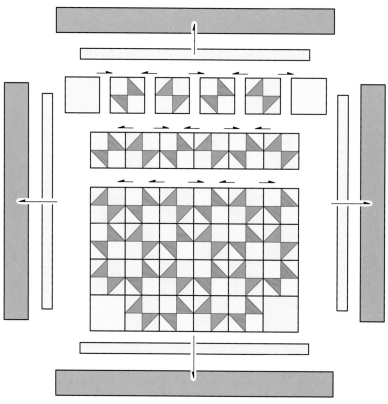

Quilt assembly